Terence Storm Publishing

Web: www.TerenceStormPublishing.com

This publication is designed as a parody and
is meant for humorous purposes only.

TITLES BY T.J. RUSS:

Everything President Obama is Doing to
Keep America Free, Strong, and Prosperous

Why Sarah Palin is the Most Dangerous Woman in America

The Audacity of Hype

Wanted: Why Rush Limbaugh, Glenn Beck, and
Sean Hannity are the 3 Most Dangerous Men in America

The Obama Border Agency

INTRODUCTION:

Are You Offended by This Book?

We hope not! This book is intended to make you laugh...
not get angry. It is a novelty product that utilizes the old fashioned
comedy of parody. This is a style of comedy that goes back to the
16th century. The Random House Dictionary of the English
Language says "Parody" is "a humorous or satirical imitation of a
serious piece of literature or writing."

Parody has been used throughout history as a fun way to
make social and political points. In today's world of dirty politics
where people say and do all kinds of very negative and offensive
things, we feel that this form of comedy is more appropriate.

So don't get angry that <u>this</u> <u>book</u> <u>is</u> <u>blank</u>. Have a good laugh.
This is the intention of this book and hopefully the person who
provided this book to you. We kept the price low, so even those who
purchased it not realizing it was a parody book would not be upset.

Besides being a fun political statement, the blank pages inside
this book can be used as a journal, sketch pad, address/phone book,
diary, or any number of other ideas. Be creative!

Finally, if you love this book and want to order large
quantities, contact the person you received this book from and ask
about discounts or visit <u>www.TerenceStormPublishing.com</u>. Or, if
you have the desire to publish your own parody book similar to
this title, visit our website for information on how we can help you
publish your own parody book at a very reasonable price.